Humble Life

Humble Life

Love Life and God. Be Humble.

Poems and Thoughts by

Raviraj Kupekar

PARTRIDGE

Print information available on the last page.

To order additional copies of this book, contact
Partridge India
000 800 10062 62
orders.india@partridgepublishing.com

www.partridgepublishing.com/india

Part - 1

Contents [Thoughts]

Poem Contents [Life's Direction]

Poems on Daily useful things in Life

Tags [Poem's]

Part -2

Content [Poems]

Content [Poems]

Part-1

O Lord

The Winds, The Trees belong to you O Lord,
Unimaginable is this, how is it Created O God....
The Feel, the Touch believes you are here,
 Heart is filled, and we have lost our fear....
The sound, the rocks behave your truthiness,
Unbelievable is this, how you created this
        oneness....
The path the way makes us you are near,
Eyes don't blink, you made us so dear...."
The rays', **The Sun** brings us your love and
        thought's,
Unforgettable is this, how this life in life
        brought....."

The Sun

One day, I asked the sun,
how much kind and humble are you...
Loving sun replied, everyone is like me,
just find son**(human)** in you, found by few...
Caring sun answered loving and helping is
    my aim,
Like humans I don't need any fame.....
Let everyone live a happy life easy and slow,
life may bring any twists, you shall see one day a
    colourful rainbow....

Human and an Ant

Human one of the wonders on planet with brain,
Ant small and simple does not give any pain…
Ant struggles and finds every way to live life,
Humans should bring love and throw every knife…
Ant travels from one place say **India** to Rome,
Ant finds every way from work to home…
Ants says and stays together and united,
Humans stop the wars or we shall become
     limited….
Universe with humans and ants stay together one,
World with rich and poor shall care and love
     everyone……….

We Indians

We people of our country,
Every thought in world makes us know,
Every great work makes India grow,
Every language makes us unique,
Every path chosen by **warriors** makes India
    antique,
Every culture makes us good,
Every Indian makes India very proud,
We the people of our country,
with good thoughts making a new entry.....

Happy and United World
Wants just one thing from every
human that is just **Truth.**

[Poems with tags -1
Back: - O Lord, the Sun, Human, India,
Ahead: - Warrior, parents, baby, grow great]

Story of a Warrior...
Great Shivaji Maharaj

Every day lived, by people of the kingdom,
Lost their belief in God, lost their freedom,
Every king came, filled pockets like hungry ruler,
Happiness was lost, every person was made a
beggar......,

Every day lived, lost their daughters and wives,
Lost trust in rulers, kingdom feared the knives,
Temples and Hearts were broken and killed,
Every River had skulls and blood was filled....,

One day came, a boy named Shivajiraje was born,
Prayers to Bhavanimata thoughts of happy
kingdom form,
Birth by**parents** Jijaaisaheb and Shahajiraje persons
of poorer,
Thought's raje gave made every heart
dearer.....,

Every mavla's trusted Shivajiraje for
creating Swarajya the Gods kingdom,

Tanaji, Prataprao, Bajiprabhu, Jadhav, Deshhmukh,
Kashid, Shinde came together for peoples
freedom......,

Forts, Durgs and Khinds fought together with
great thoughts,
Every Mavla gave blood and victory was brought.....
Tukaram, Ramdas and varkaris singed happiness
song,
Deccan, Kokan, Maharashtra wrote Rajas history
along......
Every enemy saluted Shivajis swordand word a
happy kingdom blossom,
Chhatrapati Shivaji Maharaja throne ceremony
with each mavlas(soldiers) trust was
awesome.....

Every Heart says Jay Bhavani, Jay Shivaji with love
and heart filled,
Everyone shall live good life listening to
rajas history kneeled...

Our Parents

Mother and Father an unimaginable truth given to
    us by god,
Care and happiness that they bring on earth is
    more than any thought...
May a **baby** be a girl or boy,
Every parent shall love more than any toy....
Let every human become a parent of love and
    peace,
Height any may reach the kid, parents will always
    be parents, you shall always give them a kiss....

Dear Baby

On this land you are born and you are new,
We are happy and happiness we shall give....
Care and love is always in our heart,
My Dear Sweet Baby you are a wonder and a
    God's art....
Dear, Everyday you **grow** up learn good and new,
On this Earth let's make a new world, found
    by few...
Dear, we family are there with you always for your
    future,
Together we shall make good and God's nature...

Grow Great

Great is message shouted during birth to grow,
New thoughts come to mind and you will flow,
Believe in you is the key to be good and great,
Find your own path in the group of herds,
Trust the truth and **<u>God</u>** shall help you,
The **<u>Sun</u>** shall show you the ray of hope,
Great is **<u>Nature</u>** Great shall you become,
With good thoughts you shall be someone.............

Life full of journey, **Smile at every path**
and you end your journey full of Life.

[Poems with tags-2
Back: - Warrior, parents, baby, grow great.
Ahead: - Pathfinder, God's message, nature, winds]

God the Pathfinder...

God thank you, for the path you have shown,
I have become someone from no to known,
Life is full of understanding and new paths,
You are the only one, who is the pathfinder,
Trust **God and his message** and you become the
    wonder….
God I know the wisdom you have shown to many,
Problems and struggles may come any.....
Life is full of Love and care,
Message of yours is just and just dare….
Every path will be easy and clear,
Have faith in you and have no fear…..
God thank you, for the way you give,
God thank you, on your way I and We Believe......

Sun...Gods Messenger

Dear Sun,
Gods Messenger makes everyone's fun...

Very Early we have to wake,
To make food and daily cake..
Trees and birds make a tweet sound,
Nature tell us, that God is always around....

Happy you are, happy you make,
Each night gone is daily fake...
We pray you with our heart O Sun,
With your rays, every heart be one and one.....

O Dear Sun,
God Messenger daily makes everyone run....

Nature's song

Hey Birds and Trees sing a song,

Nature sings songs of near,
Songs that ignores the past and the fear….
Sing a song with the wind,
Song sung the truth everyone shall find…

Hey Birds and Trees sing a song,

Let the God, hear you, Let the Earth, know you,
Let the Sun, clear the rust,
Let the **winds**, clear the dust,

Hey Birds and Trees sing a song.

Wind... thoughts

Wind every thought you bring,
Wind every person in this world always sing....
Wind every person you join,
Wind this thought is more than any coin,
Wind every person path you show,
Wind this thought is more wherever you go,
Wind every person you change,
Wind this thought is more than any range,
Wind wherver you go make a happy **story**,
Wind this thought shall make a new glory…..
Wind every thought you bring,
Wind every person in this world always sing....

Answer to every question is solved
whenever you never quit the question.

[Poems with tags-3
Back: - Pathfinder, God's message, nature, winds.
Ahead: -Story, truth, love, oceans]

Nature's Story...

Every tree, every bird sings a song..[1]
Feel the breeze, feel the heat,
Life is full of happiness, always dance on your feet,
Welcome you every with **truth**, for truth you
    belong....[2]

Every Leaf, every feather tells a story,...[3]
Struggle may come any, believe in your heart,
Future is yours, make a happy end that will
    become an art..
Welcome you every with peace, Nature shall help
    to make a new glory ....[4]

Truth the Life...

On the path of life,
Lord Buddha told to trust the truth…..(1)
People we become humans,
Lord Buddha gave us the **love** the fruit…..(2)
Love the loved, trust the trusted
Lord Buddha's words make us humble,
Lord Buddha's work let us sing like flute....(3)

Feel Love in every Heart.....

Winds of love, started to flow.....|1|
Rise may love in one and everyone,
Throw away knives and the gun,
Dear, always hate let away go.....|2|

Drops of love, started to feel....|3|
Oceans of love, flow in every heart,
Humility and Kindness always impart,
Dear, always fear let away kneel......|4|

Flowers of love, started to blossom......|5|
Soil grows love, grow heart in heart,
Help and smile keep everything apart,
Dear, always love, always love the world will be
        awesome........|6|

Live Life Oceans Style......

Great Ocean be the style to live in life,
Life where we have ups and downs,
Oceans water down it falls and rises high,
Higher the thoughts never will you loose,
Oceans loose the impure for pure,
Pure you become, you feel great,
Oceans greatness is to Clean,
Clean be your life with Great thoughts and **trust**,
Life is the style to live like Great Ocean'......

> **Together we can** and together lets
> be united for Love and Peace.

[Poems with tags-4
Back: - Story, truth, love, oceans.
Ahead: -Trust, life, begin, world]

Trust I say

Friend's all the best for your future,
Friends you become great by true nature,
Friends may come any problems or difficulties in **life**,
Friend might someone treat you by a knife,
Friends trust yourself and your heart I say,
Friends the world will bow you each and
    every day.....

Path of Life

Walk a Path of life to be
Kind and humble.....|1|
There may come any hurdles,
Never do you stumble.......|2|

Walk a path of life were
you become strong and bold.....|3|
The path where you find and **begin**,
Where you are more than a gold.....|4|

Plants Life...a new Beginning

Plants life, a new day in living...|1|
Every leaf grown,
Daily new way to every human being shown....
Every root water it fights,
Daily new way is seen for people's rights....
Every bird, Every ant it feeds,
Daily new **world** it shows and it leads,
Every Human that loves the Nature,
A daily good thought is a great future....
Plants Life, a new day in happy beginnings..., |2|

My Guru, My World
of Thoughts....

My thoughts of life, started to explore,
With a kind touch, guru u made me ashore...
Guru every path, made my views very clear,
Every thought of you, made me so near...

We were kids, didn't have a path........|1|
You motivated us to be kind and humble.......|2|
Inspired we were, like stone is carved......|3|
Every stroke made near guru and god.....|3|
Stopped our fear, we stopped to stumble.......|2|
We were trained, more than theories of math.....|1|

My kind views and **dream** of every Life, began to
    Flow
With a smile, guru u made me g0....
Focused are our thoughts, focused we are,
Guru our heart will love the loved, even
    you are so far.....

Patience is the Password for
the Login called Life.

[Poems with tags-5
Back: - Trust, life, begin, world.
Ahead: -Dream, destiny, way of life, travels]

Life a Dream...Be Positive

Life a Dream for every Child, a way for his thoughts,
Born with a cry, making the happy family,
Every feet it keeps, makes way to thousand paths,
Grows with an aim, with a start as an
        beginner......[1]

Every day is learned, learned with an
        understanding,
Day after day, thinking why am I different?
Why is this **destiny**, a different vision a perfect idol?
Lots of knowledge, lots of ideas helped making a
        perfect dinner........[2]

He Learns the path, path of survival of the fittest
        of all,
The path, where he falls, he stands, he learns to
        be fit,
People laugh, make fool, and then he learns the
        important ingredient,
He motivates, believes in himself, finds
        the perfect key making him true
        winner.....the positive thinker!.....[3]

Destiny in Life

On the way of life, we need a path,
Path that leads to a good person,
Person of character, lovable and humble,
Person, who helps needy, cares and is
　　trustworthy….. [1]

On the **way of life**, we come to a path,
Path that makes us think, as a good person,
Person who makes everyone near and has no fear,
Person, who cares, dares and fights for truth….. [2]

On the way of life, we make a path,
Path that everyone think, as a human being,
Person of decision, a thinker, a leader,
Person who makes a new history…..[3]

On the way of life, life finds a Destiny….

Way to Life

Life a way to understand and learn more,
Learn to find new paths and doors....
Life **travels** from good and bad,
Learn to find happiness and not be sad...

Life teaches you never ever you stop,
Learn to be positive and fight to top...
Life tells you are on top when you have love and
    truth,
Learn to believe in yourself and you find the fruit....

Life a way, happiness you shall give,
Learn life and understand everything is new....
Let your heart be kind helps needy to cure,,
Trust Life and you are always pure........

Travel a new Lesson....

Travel, Travel and get a new lesson...|1|
Share your thoughts and love,
Let the world meet you with new person..|2|

Travel shows you new ways of life and duty…|3|
Share your kindness and be humble,
Let the world and nature show you its beauty....|4|

Travel makes you happy, happiness you share…..|5|
Share the experience and the goodness of
    everywhere,
Let the world and you be together with peace and
    <u>care.</u>.....|6|

Sow a seed, plant every wood,
Let the World think of only good,
Great minds grow in every farm,
Let happy thoughts may never harm.

[Poems with tags-6
Back: - Dream, destiny, way of life, travels.
Ahead: -Care, heart, spread love, happiness]

Love and caring

Love, Love a bond of caring,
Love, Love a bond of learning....
Learn and care every **heart** every day,
Path of Universe beauty on every way.....
Ravi says, love each and every heart,
Ravi says, with Love never keep any one apart.....
Let's stop the earth from war and fight,
Let's be together and make everything right...
Love, Love a bond of sharing,
Love, Love a bond of new beginning.....

In Heart you be...

Living life always be softly….[1]
Life a way of different paths,
Path you follow spread truth,
<u>Spread love</u> and you win neatly.....[2]

People of diff thought may come
Trust yourself and strong you become….[3]
Unique heart in this world you be,
Like Fruit and Flowers from every tree….[4]

Spread Love

My Parents spoke me about the word to spread,
Son lots of hatred in this small World,
Together can we give trust and **happiness**?...[1]
Son lots of selfish people in this small World,
Together can we share belief and Truthiness?..
Son lots of inhuman done in this small World,
Together can we be humble and spread
    kindness?...[2]
Father I spoke, small the World may be,
Together we are and will always be, breaking all
    the bonds,
Spreading love, spreading love.....Togetherness,..[3]

Pursuit of Happiness...

Happiness expressed in a way,
Rich and poor be happy each and every day...
Same smile is what everyone belong,
Even ups and downs may come along...

Self-belief with truth and trust,
Every path is cleared of all dust....
Happiness pursued in such a way,
Everyone **joined together** will be its part one day....

We stay together like bees and honey,
Care and help is more than any money,
United we are like water and sea,
Love every heart, Love is the only key.

[Poems with tags-7
Back: - Care, heart, spread love, happiness.
Ahead: -Join together, work, gift, eyes]

Join People Together...

Let's join together people for good deed,
Let them aim higher for goodness our worlds
    need....[1]
Hearts and thoughts are put together,
Every soil of nation grows at any weather.... [2]
Let's join people together for good **work** and
    great aim,
Let them aim higher, for good and honest
    name..... [3]

Every day work happily...

Work every day, gives a direction,
Ravi says, any work it may be,
Work hard, and make a perfection.....||

Work for people, gives a vision,
Ravi says, any work is a **gift** you do,
Work happily, gives a satisfaction....||

Work For country, gives a motivation,
Ravi says, any work is not small or big,
Work positively, and make hearts connection....||

Happiness a God's Gift....

We are happy, belong to our inner sound,
Heart is filled, every moment is felt around.......[1]

Gone are the days, past is gone,
Present is believed, on the path along........[2]
Feel every moment of god, true gift it belong,
Gone are the days, sing happy song....[3]

Spread your happiness, spread everywhere,
True Nature is your **eyes** here and there......[4]
Let's make a true and happy world,
Your thoughts shall flow every word to word.....[5]

We are happy, belong to our inner voice,
Happiness is only just and just, is the best
        choice.......[6]

Eyes the true Wonder...

Hey you little gift, hey you little sense,.........[1]
God gifted us you, to see with an open heart,
Everyone should see a heart in heart,
Hey you little wonder, with your vision break
    every fence....[2]

Hey you little master, hey you little thing......[3]
God gifted us you n not you(blind), to make
    everyone near,
Please waste not thinking of dirty beer,
Hey you little kind, with good thoughts together
    you bring...[4]

Hey you little world, hey you little eye.........[5]
Let the Universe see the best in you,
Nature and me praise your thoughts that you give,
Hey you little Eye, with your love and thoughts the
    world fly....[6]

Think Today for better new,
Trust yourself, trust you give,
Waste not Life, goodness you make
Birth is once, only once by mistake...

[Poems with tags-8
Back: - Join together, work, gift, eyes.
Ahead: -Nature and me, Lord, Think, Back]

Farm, Nature and Me...

Sitting near Leaves of trees in a farm...[1]
I wonder never the wind blows them,
The Guts do they get,
Any situation may come, they always remain Cool
   and Calm....[2]

Sitting near Roots of Trees in a farm..[3]
I wonder never the soil sinks it,
The Strength do they get,
Any situation may come, none can harm...[4]

Sitting in a farm..[5]
I wonder never the Nature harm any, why we do?
The Heart and Feeling's we get O dear **Lord**,
Any situation may come, always be happy and feel
   charm...[6]

Lord...is One

Lord I see you, with my Heart,
Why the World not able to see you?
Give a thought, so everyone will be yours,
A thought to **think** that you are in everyone's
     hearts.....

Let the world forget the fear, forget the false,
Let the people forget the selfishness and hatred,
O Lord give a Thought where the rich, the poor,
     are one
A thought where you are we, we are everyone....
Lord I see you, let each heart feel you to be one and
     only one.....

Thinker Today

People of today need to think,
World to make a good place to live,

Good and bad are two firms,
Good is what everyone wants,
Bad removed and be deleted,

Rich and poor are just terms,
Rich has more money,
Poor's life is like a honey,

People of today need to think,

Win or lose are just paths,
Win leads to a new way,
Loosing says again you need to play,

Smile or cry you shall decide,
Smile at every path and everything is easy,
Crying shall make a person of you who is lazy…

Front or back is what you walk,
Front makes you lead,
Back tells you are in some need,

People of today need to think,
World to make a good place to live,

Never look back

On this cool and calm day,
walking the paths on every track,
In this life, full of new thoughts,
walk new way, never do you look back....
I see a squirrel, jumping tree to trees,
I see birds, adding new voice every day,
Lets learn the nature, lets love every heart,
Lets fight any hurdle, coming anyway.....
On this cool and calm day,
Never do you look back, I humbly say......

A **Friend is like an Island in a sea**, when you find the true Island you become the best sailor in the sea.

[Poems with tags-9
Back: - Nature and me, Lord, Think, Back]

Life and its Directions

Life brings us various ways and we have to decide which path I should take; we direct ourselves with various thoughts and ideas and at the end have to settle down. You should try and think for future and believe in yourselves as it said if you win you lead, and if you fail you create a path for others.......

Common Man: a true teacher

On a road I walk,
In heat and rain I travel,
I am a man everyone know in common,
I stay in a house of sand and stone,
My heart says when my family will be rich and
      happy,
I say every day when I wake up 'Come on Man'
      let's fight the day and make some money,
My Family and Friends are more important than
      honey,
People say and laugh at my work and clothes,
But I am a true **teacher,** who knows how to solve
      any question,
I am a 'Man who's always ON' to take a right
      decision,
On a road I walk,
The world will think of me when I Talk.........

Teacher: a way to trust

Teacher is a guru who thinks good of you…
Mother, Father and a Teacher is where you trust,
Your questions are answered and you are not
    turned to rust..
Become a person in few is what your guru feels,
To every answer of you is what guru deals….
Trust your sudguru (you inner soul) is what the
    guru says,
Don't waste your life in your coming days…
You are a soul to make a new **social** world of zero,
Trust your soul and you will become more than a
    hero….
Trust lies to a person you believe,

Politics: a social flame

Do you like politics is what everyone ask?
Answer to it is a difficult task...
Give and take is politics what every say,
Media fights for news every night and day..
Social work to do is what to know,
Seed for every hearts future you should sow..
Corrupt person is not whom we should blame,
Vote a right person and ignite a nation building
    flame...
Answer is now you should give,
You are the person to get elected found by few..

Agriculture: seeds of hungry

Agriculture is seen as a work of poor,
Farmer fights for market door to door…
Work one day not in garden but in a farm,
You will understand how much a farmer is cool
and calm..
Fights with heat, rains and floods,
When you eat think of his life struggle wounds
and bloods…
Eat healthy and not for taste,
Food is what never you should waste..
Farmers is one who invents food and provide us
to eat,
Let's help poor don't throw away food but put at
their feet…
You will die hungry throwing food and the fork,
Let's salute the farmer for his **nation's** work……..

Success is achieved when you are better than yesterday. Trying for the **Best within you.**

Military: service to nation

Nation to power is what military about,
Good against bad is what war is fought,
Army, Navy and Air force is what military is,
Night to day bring every human please,
War is not the only solution,
Save world from evil bravely and safely is the
    equation,
Human against human is not right,
Save truth and love and rise a new day with
    sunrise and happiness all over the **land** from
    night to light…..

Tourism: Pack your Bag's

Pack your bags and travel you think,
Holiday you want, search for something..
Sea, jungle or trek in your mind,
Family, Friends or new ones you find,
Temples and Gods you want to meet,
In your work never do you cheat,
Fun and learn you do on you tour pack,
Think of happy nation when you return back,

Service: to mankind

Help human, help needy, help for no reply,
Work for good and heaven you apply,
Care and serve good is what is your voice,
Mother takes care of her child is her choice,
Love and happy in work you do,
Fight for truth is what life says on your every
move,

Life a journey to travel,
New People you join,
Family and friends are more than a coin.

Daily useful things in Life

- Basin: Answer to every sin
- Mirror: You in You
- Toothbrush: Speak good to every
- Soap: Clean you be
- Bucket :full of strength
- Shoes :Supports You
- Bag :Happiness You Pack
- Books : Think Before you Speak

Basin: Answer to every sin

Wake up in morning for daily good,
Struggles in life for a bite of food,
Throw away your negative thoughts says a basin,
Water cleans your face,
Stronger you become in any race,
Karma says don't repeat your sin,
Answers to every question you shall get,
Patience is what **you** shall never forget…
Throw your false, Basin is one clue,
Daily think great, love and happiness you give….

Mirror: You in You

Watch in mirror who you are,
Your thoughts shall tell your travel how far,
Smile on your face is what world needs,
Your Soul is your true mirror,
Every question and answer it reads….
Trust yourself and find you in you,
Who you are, and your destiny is what, found
    by few…

Toothbrush: Speak good to every

Shine your teeth every morning,
Smoke and alcohol to health is a warning,
Let your tooth shall clean and shine,
Throw away every drug and wine,
Toxic affects your heart and kidney,
Speak good to every is a mantra leading to
    Sydney...
Toothbrush cleans daily your teeth,
Down to earth should you walk on your feet....

Soap: Clean you be

Clean is you,
Clean you give,

Soap removes dirt one by one,
Clean you are, Clean you become,
Health is important you should care,
Wealth shall come always play fare,

Clean is you,
Clean you give,

Perseverance is when you are reborn,
even when you are declared as dead...

Bucket: full of strength

Bath with cool or hot water,
Truth is what world matter,
Strong you are for every fight,
Good you and your thoughts turn everything
    right..

Shoes: Supports you

Supports you and your feet,
I shall fight with any heat,
Shoes tell you what you feel,
World is yours right you shall deal,

Bags: Happiness you pack

Pack your bags and live a happy life,
Let bags contain your work and books,
Never you deal with bad and crooks,
Bags shall bring happiness to you.

Books: think before you speak

Knowledge is what you get,
Good books make everything forget,

Think before you speak is a mantra,

Friends of needy they become,
Read Biography and you shall become someone...

Think before you speak is a mantra,

Good thoughts you shall take,
Read History and new history you shall make.....

Think before you speak is a mantra,

Ideas you get when you speak,
With good soul and thought you shall travel to a
    peak....

Think before you speak is a mantra,

Brave in life you be,
Your thoughts flow river to sea,
Fight for good is what you say,
Happy Rainbow you shall see someday....

Part-2

The King of Freedom: Kalki

World and Universe shall see a new day,
Kalki and his thoughts will show you a new way,
Kingdom of good and new,
Freedom to every he will give....|1|

Born in a family of happy and poor,
As a kid playing door to door,
Friends he made with care and good hands,
Freedom will be on every lands..|2|

Went he to a school,
Treated was he and every made him fool,
Studied good and made a new mark,
Leading to a new life and ark...|3|

Struggle in every bit of life,
Followed his way of path,
Trusted his soul and new way to lead,
Care and love is what everyone's
        need..|4|

During his studies friends were nice and good,
Finding a new way to water and food,
Good in studies he was,
Never end your life with a pause….|5|

One day he found were he is,
Fighting for life from head to knees,
He was harmed by one,
Was his aim to kill and just for fun….|6|

Kalki understood the persons aim,
He shall now show his own game,
We shall trust own soul,
Life shall show you every goal…..|7|

He works for new world,
World of humanity and humans,
Caring and loving every single bit,
            Every animal and plant,
            Every water and land….|9|

He works for good family,
Family of peace and smile every,
Fight not for money,
Saying you shall leave here every honey…|10|

Making a new world of human's,
Not with cast or color,
People joined together like a rainbow,
Everyone with unique work and thoughts…..|11|

We shall be together,
Just keep away every bad and gun,
Wars shall turn and everything will burn,
We shall be one…..|12|
Feel the heart and soul,
What it says,
Peace and harmony in coming days,
Thoughts what Kalki plays……|13|

Trust and believe the 10 Avatar,
Gods and Gurus made a master piece,
Kalki will bring love and peace,
Trust is what he wants on him…..|14|

Trust your body and God,
Toxic and drugs is not good work,
They kill you and you are none,
Don't do it just for fun...|15|

He shall solve every problem,
With sword if need,
World shall sow new seed,
Humble Life is what you read ...|16|

He shall bring new way,
Thing and believe him,
Thoughts of happy and new day,
Trust and Care him.....|17|

One day shall come,
Truth and happy is everyone,
No Politics and bad against any,
　　　　　Care to all and many..........|18|

　　　　　Kalki thoughts to thinks,
　　　　　Can the human sorted,
　　　　　With work they be hearted,
　　　　　Work shall be their name..|19|

Name they shall from work,
Nothing shall be small or big,
Same sort any in car or one who dig,
People of work we shall find.....|20|

Work shall be defined as,
Sectors that shall turn them the surname,
The work be the identity,
Today and tomorrow be the humanity....|21|

Happy with my thoughts every in future,
True be every person and culture,
Let the sun rise,
World with Kalki have freedom and be
    wise.......|22|

With new Ideas and thoughts,
Happiness is brought,
Feel good and trust you give,
World of truth found is now new.......

On this land, I shall fight

On this land,
I shall fight,
Life with lots of new ways,
I shall choose good everyday.
Struggle or Hurdles come any,
My thoughts shall touch heart of many,
On this land,
I shall fight,
Health or Care if I need,
I shall sow a good seed,
I am different from all,
My memories shall inspire and make every tall,
On this land,
I shall fight,
Bad happens if any againt me,
Thoughts I give world shall see,
On the path I walk, I shall fight,
Day after day, I and we shall make everything
        right...
On this land, I shall fight,
on this land everything will become
        alright...

Lead Life truly

One day shall come,
I shall become someone,
I shall lead or I shall follow,
Lead I shall as Leader to many,
Son or Daughter I shall care and love any….[1]

One day shall come,
I shall be someone,
I shall follow the person of truth,
Follow for the good and caring,
Black or white I shall vote and like loving…. [2]

One day shall come,
I shall be good human,
I shall now lead and follow my soul,
I shall be one found as diamond from coal,
Truth from false is life's a true goal…….. [3]

Like honey you be

Like honey you be,
With respect the world see,
Poor or rich may be one,
Humble shall you be to anyone….. [1]

Like honey you be,
With care touch every knee,
Blind or disabled be any person,
Treat same to them like your son… [2]

Like honey you shall taste,
World shall tell you are the best,
Animal or plant you should never kill,
Your thoughts shall flow and everyone kneel… [3]

Like honey you are,
Your life's destiny is not too far,
Start or end good bee your travel,
Now you honey and more than a
       marvel… [4]

Plant your thoughts..

Speak well to any, in this life,
Thoughts you share let be nice,
Your thoughts become root or leaves,
Plant your thoughts for lifecycle.....

Speak well to any, in this life,
Thought you give or take,
Plant root strong you shall make,
Plant your thoughts for lifecycle.....

Speak well to any, in this life,
Good thoughts you shall share,
Fallen leaves no one cares,
Plant your thoughts for lifecycle.....

Planned everything is....

You are just a worker,
Planned everything is,
God is the only answer think again please.....[1]

You are just a worker,
Work for good and is the only key,
With love, truth and care shall end your
    journey....[2]

You are just a worker,
Planned everything is on every route,
With faith and trust sing happy song on every
    flute......[3]

<u>Technology is built by man,</u>
Don't become servants of it,
Don't you waste your life
anyhow if you can,
Only once in a life cycle kept
on earth is your feet......

Road to take....

Thousands of way to think,
New road before I blink,
What Road should I take,
Happy many you shall make…..[1]

Many forget what to do,
Never stop and always you move,
Path you choose to be strong,
Road were you never do wrong…..[2]

Mistakes may happen some,
Never you repeat them dear son,
Life is not just a waste,
Dear believe in you and you do the best….[3]

Water to clean

Water to clean,
Hearts you shall win
Pure water you shall drink,
Peace and harmony you may bring..
Water to clean,
Free from every sin,
Water war never go on,
Happy you be from rise to dawn..

End to new

There is never an end,
Stars twinkle light to send,
New start you do is to learn,
Night after day is made by sun…[1]

Never lose hope till last,
Every frog has his bread you know,
Good thoughts is what you sow,
Life is great, happy you go…..[2]

There is always a way,
Way leading to a new play,
Preserve you should even when dead,
End to new is what god has made….[3]

<u>Lead life great,</u>
Good friends you make,
Every end has a way,
Have Smile on your face everyday...

<u>Silence Speaks,</u>
Keep cool and calm,
Everything is written on your palm,
Trust in your work and your hand,
You shall turn every stone into sand....

<u>Sun gives light,</u>
Star directs you at night,
You shall become ray of hope to needy,
Universe shall love every, I feel,
Lord shall turn everything
into goodwill….

<u>Brave you are,</u>
Travel you shall very far,
Every tree gives fruit,
Live your life true to truth,

Heart like flower,
<u>Hands of giver,</u>
True person you be,
Your Thoughts pass every sea....

<u>Humble you become,</u>
Poor or rich may anyone,
Feel your heart bit,
Humble to any you meet....

<u>When you reach on top,</u>
Never forget the help you got,
Your top will always shine,
Person who helped you
always say is mine....

<u>God you find,</u>
Always be kind,
Always god don't you ask,
Everyone gets a unique task.

Life can be defined as calculator, every calculation you make from start to stop finally will end into a zero, leaving **everything here.**

Good Thoughts should be like free flow. The amount you share good, you shall change anyone's mood. Giving many hands of food.

<u>Answer to every is beginning,</u>
Begin any of your innings,
Your life shall never end,
Till a good message of life you send.......

Big or small,
Short or tall,
Black or white,
<u>Right always for good you fight...</u>

> <u>You are creator of yourself,</u>
> Have no fear, make everyone dear,
> Beyond every boundary love
> every and be kind,
> True world and soul you shall find...

<u>Needy you help,</u>
Happy are you,
Blessing you get,
Helping never you shall forget.

<u>Become a Master,</u>
Better than yesterday,
Trust that you are unique,
Become a master piece...

<u>Think like a king,</u>
Poor and needy shall sing,
Decisions daily you take,
Family and friends happy you make.

Love each and every kid,
Person of strength for country's need,
<u>Find a true human</u> in them,
They shall fight and win every game...

Thoughts tell you were you lead,
For good future <u>plant a seed,</u>
World be free from false and bad,
Happy shall remain everyone,
never be sad…..

<u>Happy you live,</u>
Happiness you give,
After every night you rise,
Your humble thoughts
make everyone rise.

<u>We are one</u>,
United we live,
Truth we give,
Love you give everyone…

<u>Humble life you read,</u>
Answer to every if you need,
All Holy books tell the same,
Love and truth is answer to every game...

Live <u>Humble Life is a word from me,</u>
Helping poor and needy shall be the key,
After dead you, your wealth
is buried in earth,
True soul every become after birth…

Corner of world I say

In a corner of world I write,
Let my thoughts travel to every soul and every
    heart,
Every human think of light and happy every be,
Let's stop wrong, bad and every fight,

In a corner of world I say,
Throws your arms and guns,
Stop the hatred and people you fear,
Or they will die one day, and the day is near,
Let's see a rainbow smile on faces each and
    every day,

In every corner of world my thoughts flow,
Universe we create of humble and kind,
World be a safe place even for the blind,
Aliens salute the world when they come and go,

 In every corner of heart my thoughts
flow, my thoughts flow...............

Thank You and Regards
Raviraj Kupekar

About Me:-Computer Engineer and an Entrepreneur, Philanthropist having Farming backround. I Love to write Poems and thoughts for youngsters all over the universe.

I believe that everyone has his own way and will do well and best when thought positively.

Printed in the United States
By Bookmasters